The Little Flower Shop

Pluvia Bright

BookLeaf Publishing

Presentation by *BookLeaf Publishing*

Web: www.bookleafpub.com

E-mail: info@bookleafpub.com

ISBN: 9789357615778

First edition 2022

To mom and dad, for showing me how to stop
being afraid of my own shadow.

To sis-tea, for being there for me when I
couldn't be there for myself.

And to Avery - I still need to give you the
recipe for a good biriyani.

Sonder

The bell of the little flower shop jingles, and I look up from my diary. A handsome man walks in, a crooked smile on a youthful face. He is a familiar sight, lips always upturned and hair always windswept. He smiles with an ease that pulls me closer every time he returns, and I safely store the memories of them with the gardenias. I wonder after his mother when he takes home daisies.

This time, however....

He asks for a lover's bouquet, and I hastily put away the scrap of paper I was writing my number on. I put together the bloodiest roses and purest lilies and snow-flecked sky-blue orchids with blushing carnations. I wish him a good day, and watch him disappear past the geranium bushes at the windowsill.

I spend the day wondering if the lover's bouquet will find its way into the arms of an adoring wife at home, or light up the face of a lover waiting in the candlelight when the man offers him the token of love.

"I am yours," the bouquet will say, and I will my heart to hide amongst the sunflowers so the cracks can heal.
I leave the singular tear I shed in the petals of the chrysanthemums that little Sophie will come to take to her grandmother's funeral tomorrow. The woman made the best cookies in the world and her sweaters were softer than the softest rays of sunshine. I wonder if she would have given me one, Sophie's grandmother.

I don't see the man walking past iron wrought gates into the cemetery, smile vanishing with the setting sun, as he sets the bouquet on an unmarked grave, save for a heart and a single angel carving. I don't see him crying himself to sleep, hands clutching the photograph of a young man whose smile would have brightened even the droopiest of willows.

The bell of the little flower shop jingles, and I look up from my diary. A handsome man walks in, a crooked smile on a youthful face. He asks for a lover's bouquet, and this time, I place the chrysanthemum holding my tear into it at his request.
He disappears past the geranium bushes at the windowsill, and I can only stare after him in sonder.

Ephemeral

The bell of the little flower shop jingles, and I look up from my diary. A charming young woman walks past the sunflowers, and slaps down a dollar bill - she asks for a little basket of flowers.

I come alive, weaving around the aisles of flowerbeds to put together a basket as exotic as Elyn is. Lilies of the Incas and Birds of Paradise find their place next to each other, and I can see Elyn's smile grow softer as I weave together allysums and candytufts and line the basket with oxalis. Elyn kisses my cheek softly, and hurries out, petals of daffodils clinging to her blazer as the wind chime signals her departure.

Little Sophie comes by, yellow frock a sharp contrast to her mother's mourning black, yet the cheeriest buttercups wilt in her presence - she holds her hand out for a bunch of chrysanthemums, and I hand them over. I wave away the money, and her mother leaves with a grateful whisper. Sophie stops by the geranium bushes at the windowsill, and her tears still at the sight of the flowers. The pink little flowers hold not a candle to the pink of her cheeks. I smile softly, and plant some violets for her next visit.

The dull grey clouds outside deter all but an old lover and a young dreamer - then, I am left alone in the little flower shop. But I do not mind. I come alive when I give away my flowers, and I come alive when I wander amongst them too. My heart rests amongst the sunflowers, and pieces of my soul are scattered among the lavenders and peonies. A strand of my hair is buried under the dog roses, and the dirt under my fingernails has the essence of flora's bells.

Thunder crackles outside, and the bell of the little flower shop won't jingle anymore for the day. I have no more reason to pretend to be alive. I go back to my diary, and the ink seeps into my skin as I turn another page. I let the darkness take over, for I know it will disappear tomorrow when I return to silk soft petals and life giving earth. Because amongst my flowers, I'm ephemeral, but in those moments, I'm alive.

Mellifluous

The bell of the little flower shop jingles, and I look up from my diary. A little boy's laughter floats past the buttercups before he does, holding the hand of a woman with laugh lines around her eyes. She opens her mouth to speak, and I fall in love with her voice before she can tell me what she wants.

Mellifluous.

She leaves with a bouquet that has two flowers too many - a sprig of larkspur and a bloom of caladium.

Old Kevin comes in whistling a jolly tune. It's the first song he and his wife danced to at their wedding. His lips are dry and throat is parched and he asks for a single yellow tulip before going back to his off-tune melody.

Mellifluous.

I dig into the pot, the rhythmic sound of the shovel soothing to my ears as I plant ivy vines. Life giving water is next, and the gentle trickle is just another mellifluous sound in the bubble of my little flower shop.

The shutter of the shop is pulled shut, and in the silence of the night, with just the occasional honks of the sparse vehicles populating the road outside, the creak of the apartment door as it swings open is the sign that I have returned to my resting place. Not home, never home - for home is the place I just left behind.

The door of the little flower shop is propped open. The sounds of the town waking up to the rising sun is just another melody. The milkman's cycle bell tinkles as he rides past, the bottles of milk clinking against each other in a gentle chiming song. The barber's assistant has thrown open the shades, and he sweeps the front steps clean.

Mellifluous.

The bell of the little flower shop jingles, and I look up from my diary. That one sound lightens my heart and brings forth a smile nothing else can, every note of the chiming music more familiar to me than the tone of my own voice and the lines of my own palm.
Mellifluous.

Redamancy

The bell of the little flower shop jingles, and I
look up from my diary. Two young women enter
arm in arm. They're beautiful, both of them.
They both have soft smiles that glow with the
knowledge of being loved. They ask for roses,
and I pick out the fullest blooms in the loveliest
pink. They walk past the geranium bushes at the
windowsill, and I'm left looking after them,
wondering who else they could possibly give
their declarations of love to when their love was
returned to them by the person with them.

I wonder what it would be like, being loved
despite the crevices in my soul and the
death-stained skin I wore.

I seek love that loves me back. I look in the eyes
of the strangers I walk past on busy streets in
busy cities in a bustling world. I look inside me,
but all I was met with was a dark endless pit. I
look in distant jungles and in cafe windows.
During train journeys and walks along the beach
at dawn, I look for love in firefly-lit skies and
under turquoise waves.

The laburnums reach out to me, a reminder of
the darkness within me. Maybe that's what
keeps love away. I desolately walk back to my
diary. I don't see the zinnias reaching out to me,
the orange blossoms glowing softly with a light
that can light up an endless abyss. I pet my
cresses with a resignation that I'll never find a
love that loves me back.

I reach for my diary. My hands brush the petals
of a forget-me-not that lays inconspicuously by
my pen.

A reminder.

Of the memories I made in my little flower shop.
A reminder of true love.
The truest, purest love of my flowers - I look up
from my diary to see the laburnum withering
away in front of glowing orange blossoms.
Gently swaying blooms and sprigs and bushes
seem to sing to my soul.

I bring the forget-me-not to my lips, brushing
the softest kiss.

I looked for redamancy my whole life, not
realizing that standing in my little flower shop,
I'd already found it.

Zephyr

The bell of the little flower shop jingles, and I look up from my diary. A handsome man walks in, a crooked smile on a youthful face. I remember the chrysanthemum.

It's a cold day as he asks for a funeral bouquet. I add snowdrops to the bouquet before handing it to him. He leaves with a sad smile, but leaves extra change on the counter before I can stop him.

The day is a little warmer.

The sunflowers have curled in on themselves. The day is sun-warmed but still cold, and they refuse to open up. I coax open a single bloom, but the door swings open again, and it curls up into itself all over again. A cold breeze blows sprightly dandelion feathers all over the little flower shop.

The barber's assistant stands in the doorway sheepishly. He offers to sweep the floors clean of those fairy wishes but leaves with the singular

gloriosa all the change in his pocket is a few too
little to get him. I leave the dandelion feathers
scattered around - they are good luck, after all.

The day is a little warmer.

The bell of the little flower shop jingles, and I
look up from my diary. This time, it's a warm
breeze that brushes my face and all the flowers
in its wake.

The petals of the sunflowers slowly unfurl, and
turn towards the ray of sunshine who walks right
up to me. She hands me a quarter and requests a
peony. I give little Sophie seven.

She leaves a little happier than before, and the
chrysanthemums don't seem to weigh her down
as much as they did before.

And in her wake, she leaves a zephyr to dance
around the little flower shop, and the blooms
blossom in its gentle caress.

Querencia

The bell of the little flower shop jingles, and I
look up from my diary.
The man standing in the doorway is as
unfamiliar as the agave flowers. His smile
re-emerges from my memories of several
summers ago. He hands me a bouquet of scarlet
sages, and they smell like sunsets on beaches
and sandy dusks and lemony ocean waves.

He himself smells of burnt wood from the north,
with hints of the southern spices and western
perfumes. He enthralls me with stories of ships
that sailed past the edge of the world and days
spent in the wilderness.

He teaches me a new word - querencia. I can
imagine it, his mischievous blue eyes sparkling
over a mug of beer as a spanish beauty teaches
him the language of wines. His saffron scented
breath mingles with mine as he shows me the
scars he has earned from all the adventures he
has been on since he last came by.

He is still searching, he says, for his querencia.
His strength comes from people, not places, and

he is at home when he is wild, and he has never,
ever, been anything but his authentic self.

I smile and offer him a magnolia, and tell him
that perseverance is all he needs.

Silly boy. He leaves the bell of the little flower
shop jingling as he walks out and past the
geraniums. The world is his querencia, and he
doesn't even realize it.

I go to tend to my sunflowers, the restless
blooms always seeking for my attention. I water
the peonies and think about planting some witch
hazels.
In my little flower shop, I have found my
querencia.

Wanderlust

The bell of the little flower shop jingles, and I look up from my diary.

He has returned, the man with a smile a few summer memories old and a presence that reminds me of agave blooms.

He offers me a flower instead of leaving with one - a wallflower to remember him by. I let it curl up the edge of the counter.

He walks out and past the germanium, on a cold summer day, headed to wherever the wind takes him.

I remember a conversation I had with him, several summers ago. He had asked me whether I loved to wander, over waterfalls and into beaches and over forests and around mountains.

I had looked back at my flowers and answered no.

But I missed it. The days of backpacking over snow covered and laughing on the sun warmed

sands of golden coasts. I missed the world being
my oyster.
The raindrops from the edge of the sea, and
desert sunshine over rosy cheeks, and walking
through the pearl white snow under trees that
smelled of the holidays. Sweet sticky apples in
May fairs and flower fields in valleys, and
people from every walk of life - I missed being
able to feed my wanderlust.

A sprig of ivy brushes my fingertips.

I smile at my blooms and the crystal windows
and soft earth crumbles in flowerbeds. I miss
being able to feed my wanderlust, but I have a
home.
I wait for the bell of the little flower shop to
jingle again.

Arcane

The bell of the little flower shop jingles, and I
look up from my diary.

A little old woman walks in, the sunflowers
towering over her as she walks up to the counter.
She wears a little coonskin hat over her silver
hair, and her flowing pink dress puts the
carnations and roses to shame. She asks for a
bouquet to gift her son, and leaves behind a
humming song.

She calls me sweet.

Little Sophie returns alone. I see her ribboned
pigtails bobbing over the geranium bushes at the
window sill before the bell jingles, and her
smiling face walks in. She skips over to me, and
hands me a basket of apple pie. A gift from her
mother, she says, as a thank you.

She leaves after calling me the bestest florist.

A handsome man walks in, a crooked smile on a
youthful face. I remember the chrysanthemum.
He walks up to me, and asks for a lover's

bouquet. I add the snowdrops. He leaves extra change on the counter.

He calls me godsent.

They come and go, the people at the little flower shop. They come to me in times of happiness and sorrow, in grief and joy alike. They call me all-knowing, for my blooms never fail to please. Old Kevin calls me an angel.

They call me every name they can think of, from varying lips in hundreds of voices. There's one word they never call me in my little flower shop - but beyond the geraniums at the window sill....

Mysterious, they call me. They know not where I come from, whom I belong to, what I am. Unknown, they call me. Mystifying.

Arcane.

Hiraeth

The bell of the little flower jingles, and I look up
from my diary.

An old friend stands in the doorway. I can not
keep the single tear from rolling down my cheek
as I embrace her.

I shut down the little flower shop for the day,
and lead her up the stairs to my little sleeping
abode.

She tells me stories.

She tells me of emerald waterfalls under blue
sunsets and of the black marble houses I left
behind. She tells me of the little pixie garden she
started in the backyard I grew up playing in, and
of the changing autumn leaves.

It's still summer outside the little flower shop.

She asks me to return.

I think of burnt down houses, of shouted slurs,
and of hiding in the dark forests. I think of the

flowers that guided me, and the trees that
protected me.

Some places are not meant to be returned to, no
matter how much they are home.

I tell her no.

Some places are hiraeth.

Trouvaille

The bell of the little flower shop jingles, and I walk in. It's a warm autumn morning, the last summer rays falling through crystal windows.

There's a gift on the counter. It resembles a similar box, covered in similar ivies and forget-me-nots, that I received several summers before, before the man of agave blooms and the birth of sunshine filled Sophie and Old Kevin's wife's death.

In that box, there had been a key. A key to the very same little flower shop I stand in.

I know not where it came from, but it came with a note. A note that reeked of the magic I'd grown up with, and the places I'd seen.

I'd come to the little flower shop with one singular bag, and it had greeted me with open arms. The flowers seemed to bloom as I walked past them, and when
I reached the counter, the diary flipped open to greet me.

In that box, I'd found a key home.

In that box, I'd found a trouvaille.

Metanoia

In the box that reminds me of trouvaille, there's a piece of shadowed darkness.

Sunlight absorbing, depth of the void coloured stone - a shard black obsidian sits on the purple velvety cushion of the ivy and forget-me-not covered box.

It aims to protect me. From the darkness around and inside me.

It aims to purify me. Of the smoke and brine of memories whose flame lick at the edges of my mind even decades after.

It aims to help me achieve fulfilment. Psychic abilities - a bit late for that. Manifest.

It aims to change me. Transform.
Metamorphosis.

I look around my little flower shop.

I'm happy - aren't I?

I'm fulfilled and content and I have everything I could ever need. But a part of my soul clings to the obsidian. It wants to transform.

I wonder what I yearn for. Change is a constant, but the seasons and my blooms are always changing. What more change do I need?

Sweven

The bell of the little flower shop jingles, and I look up from my diary.

The people who come and go are becoming a blur. The days are growing shorter and colder, and my blooms are no longer keeping me alive. My finger tips grow cold, and my sunflowers have grown pale trying to warm me up.

The strand of my hair in the dog roses was on the floor this morning.

My soul is no longer among the peonies and the sunflowers.

My little flower shop is trying, it is. But my eyesight is growing black at the edge and my hair is burning at the ends.

I stumble into the apartment at the end of the day. As I lay in bed and the darkness takes over completely, the void gives way to pristine snow covered mountains, that smell of rain and sun and paths to the top of the world.

I fly past white peaks into purple sunsets, where
pink sands line golden oceans and orange waves.

I walk into busy marketplaces with magical
lamps and shawls and blankets made of the
colours of the wind. I see cities made of glass
and diamonds and titaniums, and countries made
of flowers and castles of cards.

I wake up with a gasp.

I wake up from a sweven.

Epiphany

The bell of the little flower shop jingles, and I look up from my diary.

It's Old Kevin with his off tune melody, and he's about to leave with his yellow tulip before he pauses. He stares into the unshed tears I am unaware of, and asks to sit down behind the counter.

I offer him a carved dark cherrywood stool. He runs a wrinkled finger under my eye, catching a tear before it can roll down my cheek, and lets it fall into the chrysanthemum next to him.

He tells me stories of the heart he lost many years prior, and of the adventures they had together. He tells me of places that seem familiar and distant and fantasies all at the same time. Of exotic tastes in intimate homes and the taste of home in foreign countries.

He tells me about the stories he writes. Of fairytales that come true and anecdotes that seem to come out of tales a dozen millenia old. He

tells me tales of bards and tales from bards and
of the history he weaves from his experiences.

It clicks.

I continue to listen to him talk about his life - a
piece of my heart sings about having found its
dream.

Apricity

The bell of the little flower shop jingles, and I look up from my diary.

Little Sophie walks past the sunflowers and the daffodils, dressed in the brightest yellow. Her breath mists in front of her as she asks for a daisy, little gloved hand handing me the money. I give her two.

The sunshine lights her way out. It's warm over icy window sills and snow covered roads, as it comes in through the crystal glass. My sunflowers bask in it, regaining some of the colour they've been losing. A dandelion turns itself towards the golden light.

It's the light that shines over frozen banks and white trees of mountains towering over raging oceans. It's the light that shines into the coldest corners of the forest, and the darkest corners of homes with crackling fireplaces and over children sipping hot chocolate and mothers knitting warm scarves for sons working oceans away and gloves for daughters whose nimble

fingers can fix any problem, and fathers who
trudge to work in its warmth.

It's winter sunlight at its brightest. It's apricity.

Novaturient

The bell of the little flowershop jingles, and I
look up from my diary.

It's the barber's assistant with a box of
chocolates in his hand. He hands it to me shyly,
and rushes away before I can thank him. It's a
goodbye gift from the barber. The dark
chocolate matches the dirt under my peonies and
lavenders, and I put it away before I get
bewitched into eating one.

Little Sophie comes by with her mother. She
offers me a toy cat, made of the softest strands
and stuffed of the plushiest cottons. It has eyes
the colour of gerberas, and a silky ribbon the
colour of sunlight.

Old Kevin drops by with the widest smile I have
seen since his heart passed away. He offers me
an old rose gold locket. It's void of any
memories, and Kevin tells me to fill it with my
own. In that little void, there are ghosts of places
from every corner of the world. I place a clover
in it.

A handsome man walks in, a crooked smile on a youthful face. He hands me a lover's bouquet. It's not from my little flower shop, and the flowers are a little droopier, but I am too busy staring at his face. He merely smiles, kisses the back of my hand, and wishes me luck.

The novaturient feeling in me grows.

The urge to leave continues to fester, and I look around my little flower shop. I lock up, and climb up to my apartment. It's time to get ready.

Resfeber

I look around my little apartment above my little flower shop. The warm wooden floor is scuffed from the time I dragged in the ancient cabinet I found in a thrift store. The old photo album I found in it is still safely stored somewhere. The pots of herbs and blooms hanging from the ceiling gently dance in the cold midnight wind, chilled by the fading winter and silver moonlight.

There's a carpet from a country with more colours than people, where spices grow more than flowers and flavour the air they breathe and path they walk on. There's an old lamp from a land of the never setting sun, and there's a pillowcase made of the softest silks the colour of magical deserts.

There are tidbits from around the world, that I have from a life past. A life I ready myself to return to. My bag is packed, and I've dug up my soul from under the peonies and lavender. My heart is still nestled amongst the sunflowers, and I trust them to take care of it while I'm gone.

If it were with me, my heart would have been racing faster than the winds that push great ships across oceans and the flutter of a hummingbird's wings. I am unaware of what the next morning will bring - it has been ages since I ventured out past my geraniums.

The resfeber tightens my throat and lightens my chest. My soul is waiting.

Des Vu

The bell of the little flower shop jingles, and I stand in the doorway.

I look around at my little flower shop.

The sunflowers where my heart still rests wave around in the breeze that moves past me. They promise to keep it safe, for they are the only ones I will ever trust it with. Petals the colour of crystallized honey turn golden in the rising morning sun, and I tear my gaze away from them.

The lavenders and peonies I buried my soul under are the colour of royal silks and purple sunsets. They glow of unearthly magic, and they promise to love the next person to find this trouvaille just as much as they do me.

The bluebells seem to tinkle with the music of pixies and fairies, and the roses are in full bloom, promises of love ready to be spread into the world.

Honeysuckle vines curl around my wrist, and I
let a sprig curl up my finger, into a ring I will
never take off. A bond of love to remember my
little flower shop by.

The buttercups and the lilacs and the jonquils
and the periwinkles and the blooms that have
protected me from the moment I stepped into
this little abode, all being to wake up in the
presence of the apricity coming through crystal
windows.

I remember the people that used to step into this
little flower shop - little children with laughs
brighter than the sunshine warming the place,
and lovers with hearts redder than the bloodiest
roses and sincerity purer than the pristine white
roses that bleed into each other. I remember old
men with jovial off tune melodies and charming
men who know the language of flower just as
well as I do. I remember the funerals and
weddings and birthdays and the everyday lives
of people I've been a part of through my
flowers, and the memories I have made.

Des vu. My little flower shop was always
another des vu.

Ataraxia

I leave behind my little flower shop.

I leave behind memories of smoke and brine and
blue fire burning along the edges of my mind.

I leave behind handsome young men with
charming smiles that were trying to forget the
soul they buried in the graveyard outside the
city.

I leave a barber's assistant without an older
sister, and a little girl without her best friend. I
leave behind old men with jovial off tune
melodies and men with smiles a few summer
memories old. I leave behind old women who
call me sweet and old friends trying to bring me
back to a home that no longer exists.

I leave behind a town that calls me arcane.

I leave behind the sunflowers protecting my
heart, and larkspurs that I used to carry in my
shirt's pocket. I leave behind a door to a little
flower shop that jingles when I open it. I leave
behind a counter with sprigs of ivy and vines

curled up the dark mahogany wood, with a little
stool carved out of cherrywood. I leave behind a
diary with ink the colour of the stone around my
neck, a little piece of darkness, still open to the
last page. I leave behind a goodbye note in my
diary.
I'm not worried. They won't understand the rest
of the pages anyways.

I leave behind a lot.

But I have a lot to look forward to. And no
matter how much I was fooling myself, my little
flower shop was my paradise and hell at the
same time. I leave it behind.

And as my little flower shop is out of sight and
so is my town, my soul is free of lavenders and
peonies. My soul is finally at ataraxia.

www.ingramcontent.com/pod-product-compliance
Lightning Source LLC
LaVergne TN
LVHW010931200726
843509LV00013B/2165